Contents

Introduction

Nearly everyone is bullied at some time in their lives: by brothers and sisters, by neighbours, by adults or by fellow pupils. If you are being bullied, you may feel scared and helpless and quite alone but you owe it to yourself to try and sort out the situation so that the bullying stops. **Remember, no-one deserves to be a victim of bullying.**

It may surprise you that all sorts of people who are now very successful adults were bullied when they were young. It is encouraging to know that it is possible to succeed in spite of being tormented at school. All of these well-known people were reported to have been bullied at school:

- David Beckham (footballer)
- Harrison Ford (actor)
- Daryl Hannah (actress)
- Michelle Pfeiffer (actress)
- Neil Kinnock (politician)
- Whitney Houston (singer/actress)
- Patsy Palmer (TV actress)
- Miss Dynamite (singer)
- Michael Grade (Chairman of the BBC)
- Victoria Beckham (singer)
- Ranulph Fiennes (Polar explorer)

- Sara Cox (DJ)
- Mel Gibson (actor)
- Tom Cruise (actor)
- Gareth Gates (singer)
- Kevin Costner (actor)

For some, the bullying went on for years; for others it was more short-lived. All of them feel that bullying is wrong and that it was not their fault, but the fault of the bully who was looking for a victim.

It is quite possible that many of you reading this book have bullied someone – perhaps a little brother or sister or a friend. Maybe you didn't mean to be a bully, but taking away that toy, or CD or not letting them play with you could be called bullying. Most of you wouldn't think of yourselves as bullies because you aren't like that most of the time. You *aren't* bullies, but you have bullied.

Some people are bullies most of the time. They make life a constant misery for their victims. I would call these people bullies and hope that they will learn to stop acting like this. If you ever bully people, then think seriously about trying to change your behaviour. It is never too late. Nobody *really* likes bullies. They may be able to frighten people into being nice to them but usually they are unpopular and quite lonely. If you break the bullying habit, you will find it much easier to find good friends.

This book will give you lots of ideas about how to stop being a victim or a bully. I hope it helps.

If you have any ideas you think would be good for the next edition of this book, please write to me and I will see if I can include them. Email: michele@kidscape.org.uk or write to me by post at:

> Michele Elliott
> KIDSCAPE
> 2 Grosvenor Gardens
> London SWIW ODH

You can also find lots of advice and information about bullying on our website: www.kidscape.org.uk

KIDSCAPE is the charity which tries to prevent bullying.

About Michele Elliott

Michele is a teacher and a psychologist. She has two sons, a husband who is a teacher and a chocolate coloured crazy cocker spaniel. She is the Director of the children's charity KIDSCAPE and has written many books and articles about bullying. She is often on television and radio.

CHAPTER ONE

What is bullying?

"Six girls in my class suddenly started being really nasty to me. They won't talk to me or sit near me. They whisper about me and make up false rumours. I cry myself to sleep."

Nina (11)

"Two older boys wait for me at the school gates every morning. They say they will beat me up if I don't give them money and if I tell anyone, they will break my arm. I'm too scared to tell anyone."

Tony (13)

Nina and Tony are being bullied. Bullying is when someone deliberately makes you miserable or threatens you. Bullying causes the victim to feel frightened and unhappy.

Are there different kinds of bullying?

Verbal

Bullying comes in many forms. Some bullies use hurtful words, like calling people fat or stupid or smelly. This is known as verbal bullying.

"She said I was ugly and looked like a pig. She made oinking noises whenever I passed by. The other kids laughed. I wanted to fall through the floor."

Vici (10)

Physical

Bullying can be physical, like pushing, hitting, shoving, kicking or punching.

"There was this one boy who always followed me home from school. He would come up behind me and push me over or try to trip me up. He shoved me into bushes and once punched me right in the face. I hardly knew him and just tried to stay out of his way. It upset me so much that I pretended to be ill so I wouldn't have to go to school."

Brian (12)

Silent

Sometimes bullying means ignoring someone, or making sure they are never included in anything. The bully might walk away or turn their back on you if you try to talk to them or they may make a rude gesture. This is 'silent' bullying – trying to make you feel bad, but not saying anything to you.

"The other kids just stopped talking to me. Any time I came into a room they all walked away. It was the silent treatment. They called it 'being sent to Coventry'. Since no one would talk to me I couldn't even find out why they were being so horrible. I had done nothing to them. It wasn't fair."

Katherine (13)

Emotional

Some bullies use the fact that someone is from a different race or culture as an excuse to bully them. Bullies may pick on people because they look or act differently or because they have a disability. Maybe the people being bullied can't read, they have a birth mark or wear a hearing aid. The bullies may use racist comments. They may say things about how stupid the kid having trouble with reading is or make fun of the person with the hearing aid. Bullies will find any reason they can. This is emotional bullying.

"A whole gang of kids surrounded me and started calling me awful racist names – too awful to repeat. They asked me why I didn't go back to the jungle and made monkey gestures and noises. Then they walked off laughing. I had never even seen them before."

Perween (10)

"When I started at my new school, this one girl took one look at me and burst out laughing. I have to wear really thick glasses and can hardly see. She thought it was great fun to embarrass me by squinting her eyes and pretending to run into walls."

Marilyn (11)

Cyber bullying

Bullies are now using mobile phones, text messages, emails and websites to attack their victims. In several cases, the bullies set up web sites and invite others to make nasty comments. This is a form of emotional bullying and is totally unacceptable.

So bullying can be anything that is done on purpose to make you feel bad when you have done nothing to deserve it.

How many people are bullied?

Bullying is very widespread. One study found that six out of ten young people said that they had been bullied. So, if you are being bullied, you are not alone.

Where and when does bullying happen?

Most bullying takes place in and around school or on the way to and from school. People I have talked to have told me that bullying at school happens in the toilets, the lunch room, on the playground or school fields and while going to classes.

Some pupils are bullied in class. Usually bullying takes place when there are no adults around, so some adults think it doesn't happen.

Does bullying really matter?

You might hear people say that all this fuss about bullying is silly. They will say things like:

"I was bullied at school and it didn't do me any harm."

This person said this with a frown on his face and a voice full of anger. He is trying to convince himself that bullying didn't bother him. If the bullying did no harm, why even bring it up? Or why not say "it did me good"? No one ever says that!

"It's character-building."

Why does someone have to be tormented in order to have their character 'built'? Character-destruction would be a better description. You can 'build' someone's character far more successfully by being kind and loving.

"It'll make a man (woman) of him (her)."

This translates as 'You only become a man when you have suffered all sorts of beatings/thefts/taunting in silence'. It's rubbish.

"There was bullying when I was at school but it didn't hurt anyone."

A comment actually made by a politician who admitted that he himself was a bully! He must have caused much suffering to his victims. I guess the bullying didn't hurt him – just everyone else.

"Sticks and stones can break your bones but names can never hurt you".

Anyone who believes this has never been called names like 'fatty', 'four-eyes', 'taphead', 'slag', 'spaz', 'Honky', 'Paki'. Names can hurt worse than sticks and stones and the hurt can last longer.

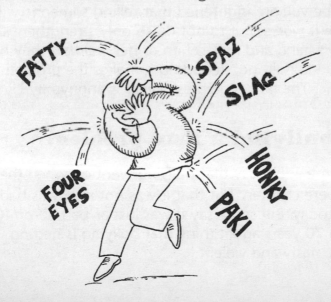

Should bullying be kept secret?

Bullying thrives in secrecy and fear. Everyone has the right to be safe from bullying and they should tell someone – it is not grassing when you are protecting yourself or someone else from bullying. Maybe you are frightened that telling someone will make it worse. But to not do so only strengthens the bully's hand and makes him or her feel that they can continue bullying. Reporting it makes the problem public. The bully's greatest shield is anonymity.

Is bullying a new problem?

Some adults say that bullying went on when they were children, but that it was not nearly as bad as it is today. But some say it was just as bad 30 or 40 or even 70 years ago. I think that bullying is getting more nasty and violent.

"At first it was just name calling, then it got worse. The three of them would follow me home and kick or punch me. Once, they shaved off my hair. Another time they threatened me with a knife. When they put dog mess through my letter box, my dad found out and called the police. It stopped after that."

Ian (12)

Do boys and girls bully in the same way?

In the past we thought that boy bullies were likely to use physical kinds of bullying and girls more verbal or emotional kinds of bullying. Lately we are seeing more girls using physical bullying.

"My friend Susie was beaten up by a gang of girls. She had her nose broken and ended up in hospital. The gang got in trouble with the police and they all got kicked out of school. Susie's fine now, but I couldn't believe that girls could act like that."

Lisa (14)

What is the difference between teasing and bullying?

When I was a child, there was a lot of teasing in our house. It was always in good humour and we all enjoyed it and joined in. Whenever the teasing got out of hand, it was instantly stopped by my grandmother. It was definitely not bullying and it did give me a good sense of humour.

The rules for teasing are simple:

- teasing is between people who like each other
- teasing is only allowed when everyone is having fun
- teasing is stopped as soon as one person feels unhappy

"My sister and I tease each other all the time. I tell her she is a creepy little airhead and she tells me I am a vampire weirdo, all in fun. We do fight and sometimes I think she's a bully, but we work it out."

Paul (16)

"The trouble with teasing is that my little sister is great at dishing it out but she doesn't like to be teased herself. I don't think this is fair, do you?"

Maria (13)

No, I don't think it is fair. Teasing has to go both ways or else it's bullying. One thing I would have to ask Maria is if she is teasing her younger sister in a way that is too grown-up for her, so she can't really tease back. Maria needs to look at how she is teasing her and if it is the same way she is being teased, then her sister needs to learn to play fair. Otherwise, Maria should just walk off and not let her sister tease her.

Isn't bullying just normal human nature?

Bullying is wrong and should be stopped. Why should anyone be picked on? Bullying is not normal human nature. I certainly know hundreds of people who do not bully others, so if it is part of human nature I guess they aren't human!

Remember

- No one deserves to be bullied.
- No one should ignore bullying
- Bullies who get away with bullying learn that it is a good way to get what they want. They grow up to be big bullies.
- Bullying is always cruel, whether it is name-calling, exclusion from the group, hitting or making some one do something they don't want to do.

What if?

What If? questions can help you think about what to do if ever anything should happen to you. There are no right answers because every case is different. Look at the questions with your parents or with friends and decide what you think might work. Think of your own solutions and make up new What If? questions to answer.

Helen is in the school playground, minding her own business, when an older girl, Lisa, accidentally trips her up. Helen falls over and bruises her knee. Should she:

a) Hit Lisa hard?
b) Give her a chance to apologise?
c) Sit down and cry?

Give Lisa a chance (b). If it was an accident, then she should say sorry. If it hurts, I think Helen can go ahead and cry! But if it wasn't an accident, tell someone — and try not to cry in front of the bully; that could make matters worse.

Whenever Sophie has the chance, she makes rude comments about Rosemary. She calls her "smelly, ugly, pimple face, stupid" and anything else she thinks will hurt her feelings. Sophie always chooses her times so that Rosemary

and the other kids hear, but the teacher doesn't. Last week, Sophie started texting hurtful names to Rosemary. Rosemary is getting more and more upset by all this. Should she:

a) Ignore the comments?
b) Confront Sophie and tell her off?
c) Tell the teacher?
d) Punch Sophie in the nose?

Rosemary must feel like punching the bully in the nose but she'd probably get into trouble if she did. Bullies seem to be quite clever at not getting caught, while victims often get caught when they fight back. Rosemary should try (a) first – ignore the comments and pretend that it doesn't bother her. Sophie might get tired of bullying her if she doesn't get angry or cry or react. It seems like this has been going on for some time, though, and perhaps it is time that the teacher is told (c) about the comments. If Rosemary feels brave, she may try telling the bully off (b). It might startle her into silence. Rosemary should keep the text messages and show them to either her parents or the teacher. This is proof that Sophie is bullying her. Sophie's parents should be shown the messages so that they and the teacher can help her change her behaviour.

CHAPTER TWO

What can I do if I am being bullied?

"If you are being bullied, make sure you talk to someone about it. Don't keep it to yourself! Tell a friend, a teacher or your mum before it gets out of hand. The phrase 'a problem shared is a problem halved' is very true."

Emma Bunton

"I am small for my age and I have just started secondary school. I have only been there for a month, but an older boy has started to pick on me. At first it was just a few comments about my ears, then he started tripping me over, punching me on the arm and taking my dinner money off me. I don't want to be a baby, but I can't take much more."

Andy (12)

Ask a teacher if your school has a way of dealing with bullying. It should.

For example, some schools:

- have anti-bullying guidelines and procedures for dealing with incidents
- encourage anyone who is being bullied or who witnesses bullying to tell a member of staff about it
- have 'bully boxes' where students put in a note about what is happening
- have student meetings, circle time or 'courts' where problems like bullying are discussed and dealt with
- have specially trained students to help each other or teachers who are chosen to help

"We have assemblies about bullying every term and we do lots of stuff about it in class. Not much bullying goes on here now – everyone knows they get in trouble if they try to bully. I hope my next school is as good."

Dan (11)

If your school has an anti-bullying system, use it to get help. If you're not sure how it works, talk to your teacher or Head of Year.

If your school ignores bullying, *don't accept that you have to be a victim.* You can still help yourself and you can ask others to help you.

- **try to ignore the bullying or say 'No' really firmly, then turn and walk away.** Don't worry if people think you're running away. Remember, it is very hard for the bully to go on bullying someone who won't stand still to listen.

- **try not to show that you are upset or angry.** Bullies love to get a reaction – it's 'fun'. If you can keep calm and hide your emotions, they might get bored and leave you alone. As one young person said, "They can't bully you if you don't care".

- **don't fight back, if you can help it.** Most bullies are stronger or bigger than their victims. If you fight back, you could make the situation worse, get hurt or be blamed for starting the trouble. It's not worth getting hurt to keep possessions or money. If you feel threatened, give the bullies what they want. Property can be replaced – you can't.

- **think up funny or clever replies in advance.** Make a joke of it. Replies don't have to be wonderfully brilliant or clever but it helps to have an answer ready. Practise saying them in the mirror at home.

Using prepared replies works best if the bully is not too threatening and just needs to be put off. The bully might decide you are too clever to pick on.

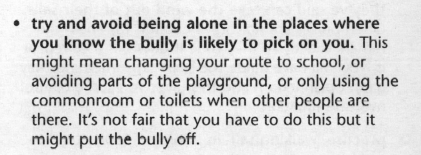

"I was always bullied about my glasses. By the time I was 11 I was desperate. Then my dad helped me think up some replies. It felt stupid saying them out loud at home and I didn't think it'd work. The first time I tried one of them out, Paul – the bully – was so surprised, he backed off. Everyone else laughed with me – not at me."

Martin (13)

- **try and avoid being alone in the places where you know the bully is likely to pick on you.** This might mean changing your route to school, or avoiding parts of the playground, or only using the commonroom or toilets when other people are there. It's not fair that you have to do this but it might put the bully off.

- **stick with a group, even if they are not your friends.** Bullies tend to pick on people when they are on their own. If you have a friend you can confide in, ask him or her to help you. It will be harder for the bully to pick on you if you have a friend with you for support.

- **sometimes asking bullies to repeat whatever they've said can take the wind out of their sails.** Often bullies are not brave enough to repeat the remark exactly so they tone it down. If they repeat it, you will have made the bully do something they hadn't planned on and this gives you some control over the situation.

- **practise 'walking tall' in a mirror.** Bullies tend to pick on people they think are weak or timid and they often think shy, quiet people make easy targets. *If you look positive and confident, the bully will find it harder to pick you as a target. Pretend — even if you only feel two centimetres high inside.*

- **try some of the assertiveness techniques in chapter four.**

- **keep a diary about what is happening.** Write down details of the incidents and your feelings. When you do decide to tell someone, a written record, including text messages, emails or anonymous phone calls, makes it easier to prove what has been going on. Contact your Internet Service Provider (ISP) for advice.

- **tell your parents or other adults** – you need their help. Don't suffer in silence.

Why am I a victim of bullying?

It's hard to say why someone is picked out by a bully. If you aren't doing something anti-social like picking your nose or clucking like a chicken, then it isn't your fault. Basically, the bully needs to have a victim – any victim – so he or she might choose anyone and then decide what to bully them about – looks, brains, race, family etc. The bully will keep going on any issue until they get a reaction. Then they will keep on bullying you about whatever it is that bothers you.

You might just be in the unlucky position that you were in the wrong place at the wrong time. Most victims of bullying are sensitive, intelligent and gentle. They've done nothing to deserve being bullied. Most get on well with their parents. They don't come from families full of conflict and shouting, so when bullies attack them, they do not know what to do.

The sad fact is that, from the bully's viewpoint, people like this make excellent targets because they are nice and won't fight back. They might even cry, a bonus for the bully. If you could point out one 'fault' of these victims, it would be that they are too nice!

"Jennifer seemed to find it fun to bully me, even though I tried to be nice to her. I asked her why she did it, and she just shrugged and said that I was too nice and it was sickening. I was so hurt that I cried and that made it worse. It went on for two years until she moved."

Leila (10)

It is the bully who is the problem. But, if you think you might be a bit too sensitive, work on toughening yourself up. Follow some of the suggestions in the assertiveness chapter which starts on page 58.

What if a gang is bullying me?

If you are being bullied by a gang or if you've been sent to Coventry, get the weakest member alone or phone him/her at home and ask them why you are being bullied. This is easier if you know the person and have some sort of relationship with them.

- ask them how they would like to be treated as badly as you are being treated
- ask why they are joining in
- say you know that they are not really cruel underneath – appeal to their good side

Often members of a bully gang join in to keep on the gang leader's good side. They wouldn't go along with the bullying if they had a choice. If you talk to the nicer gang members on their own, you might be able to get some of them to stop, or you might be able to get help together.

"I was really scared before I rang the girl I know in the gang. We talked a bit and then we met some of the others. I thought they all hated me but they said they felt bad about all the things they'd done. Things got better after that."

Ellen (11)

Some bullies are brave in front of friends but on their own they feel weak and uncomfortable. If you think the person bullying you needs a gang for support, try and get them alone – they are likely to be much less aggressive and you might be able to talk about how to stop them picking on you.

"I was bullied by a boy called Pete – he had a gang of about four or five and they used to corner me in the toilets or changing rooms. I was scared for months. Then I met Pete on his own outside school. He made some sarcastic comment – I went berserk. I yelled at him. Seeing him on his own gave me the courage I needed to say all the things I'd wanted to say for ages. He tried to ambush me with his gang in school after that but I wasn't having it – I'd seen through him."

Malik (14)

If the gang is beating you up or taking your money or making threats against you, then you must tell your parents and perhaps the police. It may be that the gang is already known to the police if they are threatening people outside the school.

Who can I tell if I'm being bullied?

"This boy keeps bullying me because I don't want to be his girlfriend. He makes comments about what I wear and is sarcastic all the time. He won't leave me alone, but maybe telling will make it worse."

Dee (13)

Usually it's difficult to sort out the bullying on your own or even with the help of friends. You should think seriously about telling an adult. It's the only way to get the bullying stopped.

If you need adult help, don't be embarrassed about asking. Everyone needs help sometimes and asking for help to stop bullying doesn't mean that you are weak or a failure.

Telling someone about bullying isn't 'telling tales' or 'grassing'. You have the right to be safe from attacks and harassment and you should not be silent when you are being tormented and hurt.

Often people don't tell anyone about bullying because they are frightened that the bully will find out and things will get worse. This is a natural fear but schools can put a stop to bullying without the bully learning who reported it. It's also more than likely that the bully is picking on other people as well as you, and won't know which of them was brave enough to reveal the truth.

Even if the bully does find out, it is better to have the situation in the open. Bullies depend upon secrecy.

"I told a girl in the Sixth Form that I had been 'sent to Coventry'. It was so hard because I had just got to secondary school and I was unsure of what to do. This girl said it had happened to her too. She and some other Sixth Formers talked to the bullies. I was scared about what they would do but they'd obviously been told they were well out of order and the bullying died out."

Tracy (12)

Parents

"My life was literally hell for three years, ever since I started secondary school. I don't know why I waited so long before telling my dad about the bullying. He really made the school sit up and take action."

Mark (now 15)

- **talk to your parents about the bullying.** They may have sensed that something is wrong already, or they may have noticed that your possessions or money keep vanishing. There is a great deal they can do to support you.

Parents can talk to a teacher or your Head of Year or Headteacher. Most schools take what has happened very seriously. Parents can say to the school that:

- Bullying at school is not the victim's problem: it is a school discipline problem, and the school should be prepared to stop it.
- The school should be able to give you and your parents details of how they handle bullying and their anti-bullying procedures.
- They want to know what the school is going to do to protect you from the bully.

If the bullying continues, your parents can make a formal complaint to the school governors or to the Local Education Authority.

"When I told my dad that I was being bullied, he just said I should go and hit the bully. My mum didn't agree and my parents ended up fighting all the time. I was sorry I said anything. In the end the only person who really helped was my PE teacher. Other parents seem to help their kids, why didn't mine?"

Josh (14)

Poor Josh. Unlike Mark, telling his parents did not help. In some families the bullying affects more than the child, it affects everyone – mother, father, brothers and sisters. If you are in a family which can't cope with the bullying, or which does not seem to care about your problems, then do get help from someone else like a school nurse, teacher or a friend. Or ring one of the helplines listed at the back of this book. There are numbers your parents can call for help, too.

Teachers and schools

"It got so bad that I used to cry myself to sleep every night. I hated school and was scared to tell anyone about the bullying. It was just two girls, but they followed me everywhere and made fun of me all the time. My friends said to ignore them, but somehow you can't. They really got to me. One day at lunch I started crying and one of the dinner ladies talked to me. I told her everything and she helped me talk to my teacher. I didn't know what to do. Now it's better. The bullies aren't my friends, but they leave me alone."

Mary (10)

- **if you don't want to talk to your teacher, there are other people in the school who might be able to help:** playground supervisors, dinner staff, Year Tutor, Head of PSHE, nurse, secretary, or any member of staff that you like.

- **write it all down** in a letter if you can't face telling someone. Send or give the letter to them with your diary and keep a copy yourself.

- **explain what is happening and who is involved.** You might want to take a friend with you, especially if they have witnessed some of the bullying incidents. Show your diary.

- **make sure you explain how bad the bullying is making you feel.** Sometimes people don't understand how hurtful name-calling and verbal abuse can be. Make it clear that you are extremely upset by it and want it to stop. See page 62 for some ideas about how to express yourself clearly.

- **school staff should make sure that pupils are safe when they are in school.** Find out how they are going to help. You could suggest that students have lessons about bullying, or that teachers introduce bully boxes for reporting incidents, or have specially trained students other pupils can talk to. You may have your own ideas.

School Phobia

"I am terrified of going to school. I shake whenever we get near the school. I can't go into the school gates without crying. The bullies see me crying and that makes it worse. My mum says I have school phobia and that I need counselling. What is school phobia?"

Henry (10)

A phobia is an overwhelming fear of something. Some people have a phobia about spiders or snakes or high places. It seems that you have developed a phobia about school because you were badly bullied. Have your mum contact your doctor and one of the help organisations at the back of this book. You can overcome this, but you will need help. I would like to know what the school is doing about the bullies!

Changing Schools

If the bullying is unbearable and the school can't or won't do anything about it, talk to your parents about going to another school. **Never feel that there is no way out.** It is even legal for you to be educated at home and not have to go to a school at all.

> "I was worried that going to a new school would be just as bad as my old one where I was bullied by this group of kids. But the new school doesn't have much bullying at all and the teachers are brilliant; you can tell them anything. I have new friends and I am glad I left. My friends at the old school say that things are still bad there and the bullies are bullying other kids."
>
> Melissa (10)

Changing schools won't necessarily solve all your problems automatically, and you should try to tackle the bullying if you can, but don't ever feel you are trapped in a hopeless situation. It is always worth talking about other options.

What can I do if I am being bullied by a teacher?

> "My Maths teacher always used to ask me questions which he knew I couldn't answer. He'd laugh when I didn't know and everyone else joined in – I cried after every lesson."
>
> Barbara (13)

Teachers and members of staff are there to help you learn and to support you. If you are a constant nuisance, disruptive or inattentive, teachers will tell you to stop. This is part of their job.

However, if you are doing your best and a teacher or other member of staff continually picks on you, humiliates you in front of others, or taunts you, then you are right to complain.

Talking to your parents about what is happening is the best way to deal with a teacher or staff member bullying you. They can go to the school on your behalf. But you could also try to do something about it yourself:

- keep a diary of the dates and what happened when the teacher or member of staff bullied you and list the names of witnesses. Write down exactly what happened and how you felt. If you can, tell your parents and ask them to talk to the Headteacher.
- the teacher may not realise what he or she is doing. If you feel confident enough, ask to see the teacher, (with your parents) and discuss how they are making you feel. In some cases this can work – for example, a new teacher might not know how his or her comments are affecting students.
- talk to your Headteacher in confidence about the teacher or staff member who is bullying you and ask for advice and help.
- you can ask to be moved to another class, if possible, or even ask to change subjects if the situation cannot be resolved.
- write a letter to the teacher explaining how you feel. Even if you don't send it or show it to anyone, it will help you to get your feelings out. The letter might be a good way to let the school know what has happened. Your parents could use it when talking to the teacher or Headteacher.
- if all else fails, your parents could make a formal complaint to the school governors or you could move schools. Hopefully it will not come to that.

Remember, you don't deserve to be bullied by anyone – adult or child.

What about suicide?

"Whenever I hear about someone my age committing suicide because of bullying, it scares me because I have thought about it myself. I started collecting tablets when the bullying got really bad. I thought it would be better to die. Do other kids have the same thoughts? Am I mental?"

Gemma (14)

G emma wrote to me after another 14-year-old girl took her own life. Of course she is not mental! And other kids do have the same thoughts. I know that people who are bullied think about getting away from it and sometimes suicide seems to be the answer. It isn't. There are better ways to cope as I hope this book will show you. You do not have to put up with the pain of bullying, but you do not need to kill yourself. I have met and talked to the parents and brothers and sisters of young people who have committed suicide. They never get over it and are in so much pain that I know the person who died would never have done it if they had known the anguish. One mother said she wanted to die, too.

Suicide only causes more grief and means the bullies have won. Don't think that they will be sorry, some of them will just laugh. Remember the people like Tom Cruise and Miss Dynamite, Kevin Costner and David Beckham, all of whom were bullied but went on to prove that they could have better lives than any of the kids who bullied them. Who ever heard of the people who bullied them? No one.

If you ever think of suicide call The Samaritans or ChildLine or Kidscape – all of the numbers are at the back of this book. Don't ever let bullying get that much on top of you. There are people who will listen and help.

Anorexia and Bulimia

"I used to be chubby and these girls called me fatty and Miss Piggy, so I went on a diet and lost lots of weight. Now I am thin I can't seem to stop dieting. I go to the toilet and throw up whenever I eat at home. At school I don't eat at all. I think about food all the time, but at least the bullying has stopped. I saw a programme on television about anorexia and I think I am getting it. What should I do?"

Joyce (13)

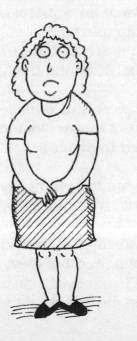

Joyce needs to get help immediately. She is in serious danger of starving herself. The first person she should tell is her mother or father and then go to see her doctor. If you or a friend have this problem, you can also contact the organisations at the back of this book. Don't wait for a minute, get help now.

What can I do if I think a friend is being bullied?

People who are being bullied might not report it, but they may show behaviour that gives us a clue to what it is happening. There may be other reasons they act like this, but watch out for bullying if someone you know:

- is frightened of walking to or from school or changes their normal route to school
- does not want to go on the school bus
- is unwilling to go to school at all and truants or feels ill every morning
- begins doing poorly in their school work
- has their clothes or books or homework torn
- is nasty to friends or family (perhaps because they feel so bad)
- is starving at lunch time, but has no money because the bully has taken their dinner money
- becomes withdrawn, or starts stammering
- becomes distressed and anxious, or stops eating
- refuses to say what's wrong (because they're frightened of the bully)
- has unexplained scratches, bruises, etc.

"I was frightened to tell anyone about the bullying, but I started being horrible to everyone. I guess I hoped someone would notice and ask me what was wrong. The bullying happened on the school bus, so I begged my mum to drive me. She wouldn't, so I was late every morning and missed the bus. I also wet the bed a couple of times. I was so ashamed. Here I was, 13 years old and wetting the bed. The bullies would have loved it if they had known."

Emma (14)

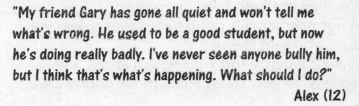

"My friend Gary has gone all quiet and won't tell me what's wrong. He used to be a good student, but now he's doing really badly. I've never seen anyone bully him, but I think that's what's happening. What should I do?"

Alex (12)

There may be a lot of reasons why Gary has changed. Perhaps there are problems at home or he has some other concerns. But, if you are good friends, I suggest you tell him you think he is being bullied and you want to help. He may tell you and then you can go together to a parent or teacher and get help. He may deny it, out of fear. If he does, say that you are always there and he can talk to you anytime. If you are really worried, get some advice from an adult or ring one of the helplines listed in the Resources section on pages 110–4.

Cyber bullying

If bullies are using text messages, emails or websites
to bully you:

- change your mobile phone number – only give it to
  family and trusted friends
- keep a copy of anything sent to you and a note of
  the date and time it was sent. You may wish to
  make a formal complaint to the police.
- contact your Internet service provider to find out
  how they can help block messages
- do not open emails or text messages unless you
  know who sent them
- tell your parents and your school about any
  websites, emails, texts, anonymous phone calls.

Remember

- Not to think like a victim.
- To always report bullying and get help – it is
  difficult to solve bullying problems by yourself.
- Telling about bullying isn't grassing – it's self
  protection.
- Lots of famous people were once bullied and
  they went on to have fabulous careers and
  happy lives.

What if?

Anna is in the school toilet standing at the sink when an older student, Emma, comes in, pushes her around and then punches her. Anna hardly knows Emma and asks her why she's picking on her. All Emma says is "shut up and don't tell or I'll really hurt you next time". Anna feels afraid, but angry as well. Should she:

a) Wait until Emma leaves and then tell a teacher?
b) Get in a fight with her?
c) Accept what has happened and not report it?

Anna didnt deserve to be punched and the bully was wrong to do it. She should report it, (a) – if she doesn't the bully will just keep on bullying and beating up other kids.

Jenny, age 11, hates school. Her parents have split up and neither her mum nor dad can keep her or her younger sister. Jenny lived for a while with an aunt and uncle, but the uncle was horrible to her so she ran away and never told anyone why. Jenny was finally taken into care and now she is at a new school where she doesn't know anyone. She likes her foster family but misses her old friends. A group of girls in her new school call her names, tell her she is a 'black crow' and that her parents don't want her because she is mixed race. They tell the other girls not to play with her. They tell her that if she tells, they will beat her up after school. Jenny is terrified and miserable. What do you think she should do?

a) Not tell anyone and suffer in silence?
b) Go up to the girls and threaten to beat them up if they don't leave her alone?
c) Try to ignore them until they just give up?
d) Tell her foster mum or someone in the family?
e) Tell a teacher she trusts at school?

My advice is not to suffer in silence – that just gives the girls more power and they will continue to be nasty. Jenny can try ignoring them, but if that doesn't work she should tell either her foster mum or dad or a teacher at school.

Also, Jenny has suffered not only from verbal bullying and racial abuse from the girls, but also she has no real help from her family. She will need to talk about the bullying to someone when she is ready. She can ring one of the helplines listed at the back of this book or tell a trusted adult like a teacher or social worker, but she should try to get help.

CHAPTER THREE

What about bullies?

Phil Collins, the singer, has strong feelings about bullies. He says: *"If you can understand that bullies are sad people who can only make their presence felt by making others suffer, and whose actions tell us loudly that they are lacking in other areas of life, only then can you find the strength of mind to survive these bullying encounters and move on with your life – something it is highly unlikely that the bully will ever do."*

"I was the biggest bully in school. I thought it was cool that everyone was scared of me. I know now that I was acting that way because I felt so bad about myself. I wish I could go back and do it all right, but it's too late now."

Gita (18)

People become bullies for lots of different reasons:
- they are being bullied themselves
- they are selfish or spoilt and always want to get their own way
- they have no friends and feel lonely
- they feel bad about themselves and they want to make others feel bad too
- they are taking out their own frustration on others

- they have family problems
- they feel insecure and unimportant – bullying gives them power
- they want to look 'big' in front of others
- they have been bullied into joining a bully gang and have gone along with things just to keep on the bully's good side
- they don't understand how bad victims feel
- they want to be in control of everything
- they enjoy the feeling of power
- they have got away with bullying for so long they think no one can stop them

Whatever the cause, bullying is usually a signal that the bully needs some help.

Bullies need victims. The bully will always be able to find something about a person to focus on: wearing glasses, having 'big ears', being in a wheelchair, being good at exams, or too small and shy, too fat, too thin, too attractive, too intelligent, too creative, or being the 'wrong' colour or wearing the 'wrong' clothes.

Bullies use 'differences' as an excuse for their bad behaviour. But it isn't this 'difference' in the victim which causes the problem – it's the bullies who have the problem because they are:

- afraid
- envious
- angry
- unhappy
- jealous
- cruel
- insecure
- thoughtless

Differences make people interesting and unique.

Lots of famous people who were bullied were 'different' – they turned out to be more talented and successful than any of the people who bullied them. People like Gareth Gates, Harrison Ford, David Beckham, Sara Cox, Ranulph Fiennes and others succeeded in spite of being tormented. I wonder what happened to the bullies...?

"There was one bloke who really annoyed me – he had a funny high-pitched voice and he jumped even if you just said hello. We hid his stuff, pushed him out of queues, and everyone knew better than to talk to him. We just did it for a laugh. I suppose he must have hated us. I wouldn't blame him. We were awful."

Jake (16)

What's the thrill of bullying?

"I loved being a bully. It made me feel important. I could do whatever I liked and no one dared to stop me."

Steve (12)

Bullying makes bullies feel powerful and in control. Most bullies know exactly what they are doing. There are times, however, when the bully doesn't know how much harm she or he is causing. Perhaps they go along with the crowd and say hurtful things without thinking through what they are doing. Perhaps they bully because they are secretly frightened that if they don't, they will be the next victim. Perhaps they bully because they are bored. Whatever the reason, it is no comfort to the victim whose life has been made a misery.

What happens to people who are bullies?

"I'm in a young offenders' institute because I was caught mugging an elderly lady. I've been thinking that maybe I wouldn't be here today if someone had stopped me from being the biggest, meanest bully in school. Everyone, including the teachers, was scared of me and I loved it. I see my younger brother doing the same thing now and I guess he'll end up like me. I wish I could talk some sense into him. Could you please send me anything you have that might help me to save him?"

Dominic (17)

I wrote back to Dominic with some suggestions, but if his brother isn't stopped, I'm afraid that he, too, will be headed for a criminal record and jail. A study by a man called Dan Olweus in Norway found that boys who were bullies at age 8 were four times more likely to end up in prison than non-bullies. The charity KIDSCAPE talked with boys like Dominic in two young offenders' institutes and found that 9 out of 10 had been involved in bullying while at school. Of course, kids who are bullying seldom think about what will happen if they continue to act like thugs and not all bullies end up in prison. But it would seem that there might be a link between bullying and your chances of ending up in serious trouble with the law.

I sometimes bully people. What can I do?

"I guess I've always been a bully. My sister bullied me all the time and it seemed a good way to get my own back. I know that my friends only hang around me because they are afraid I will turn on them. Sometimes I feel really bad about the way I act, but I don't know how to stop."

Debbie (10)

ost people have bullied someone at some point in their lives but they usually feel sorry about it afterwards and try not to do it again. However, if you are constantly picking on other people and you don't care how angry or upset you make them, then you've got a problem.

Admitting that you sometimes bully other people can be hard but we all have to face up to what we do and how

we make others feel. No one really likes bullies.
If you want to be liked for yourself, then you should try
to change the way you treat other people. Bullies might
frighten people into being nice to them but this isn't
friendship – bullies are usually lonely and unhappy.

**If you are a bully, then you can change – even if
you like yourself as a bully!**

First of all, try to work out *why* you bully others:

- **do you mean to upset or hurt others?** When you
  talk to people do you want them to feel small and
  intimidated?

- **do you bully people without realising** – is it only
  people's reactions which tells you that you have
  done something wrong?

- **is something making you miserable?** A problem
  at home or at school?

- **do you feel left out or lonely at school?** Do you
  think people are avoiding you or are just friends
  with you so you won't bully them?

- **is someone picking on you?** A teacher, another
  adult, someone in your family, another pupil? How
  does this make you feel? Do you take your bad
  feeling out on someone else? Could you try to talk
  to this person to see if you can sort out the
  problem yourself? Could someone else talk to them
  for you?

- **is there a particular person that you pick on?**
Why do you target him or her? Are you jealous or
envious of them? Do you think this person is a
wimp? If there is someone who really bugs you, try
to stay out of their way. If you can avoid them, you
won't have a chance to wind them up.

*"We thought one girl in our year was fat – she probably
wasn't really, but we went on and on at her about it. She
suddenly started to lose weight and then we found out
that she had become anorexic. In the end, she had to go
into hospital. I feel ashamed about it now."*

Meera (13)

- **do particular occasions irritate you** so that you
take out your feelings on others? Can you pinpoint
exactly what annoys you the most – could you
change whatever it is? Try to think of ways to avoid
these situations in future or make up your mind
beforehand that if you do get caught up in them
again, you'll walk away before you say or do
anything you might regret.

- **does something (a particular lesson or task)
make you feel angry or frustrated?** Do you find
some subjects really hard? Can you talk to someone
about the problem?

- **do you feel that you are letting someone down**
by not being clever enough, or talented enough, or
polite enough? Sometimes families or teachers can
set such high standards of achievement that we feel
we can never match up to what they expect of us.

This can be very demoralising. Often these people don't realise that they are putting such a burden on us. If you feel like this, try to talk to them about it and explain how you feel.

- **do you go round with a gang which bullies people?** Why do you stay with the gang? Do you really want to be with people who are always picking on others?

"I suppose I just messed around most of the time at school. I had a couple of mates and we used to make the younger kids pay us every week or we'd give them a right kicking. We must have been pretty frightening. None of that's much good to me now."

Darren (16)

- **do you get a thrill from hurting other people or taking their things?** Does this make you feel powerful?

- **are you bigger and stronger than other people your age?** Do you use your size and strength to intimidate others?

- **do you identify with violence and cruelty?** Why? Were or are you the victim of violence? If so, you can break the cycle of violence and make sure no one has to suffer like you did.

Is there someone you trust that you could talk to about the problem? Discussing things with someone else often helps to make them clearer. It can be hard to change ingrained habits and having someone else on your side will make things easier.

"I didn't know how bad victims felt until my brother was bullied. He's 3 years younger than me and he has to wear a hearing aid. The bullying he went through made him into a wreck until we got it stopped. I realised I'd made kids feel like that. I wouldn't bully anyone now."

Rob (13)

How can I stop being a bully?

"Bullying is evil. If you bully others it will always come back to haunt you."

Frank Bruno

"My dad is a horrible person. He gets drunk and hits us for no reason. I couldn't tell anyone or it would just get worse. I think that's why I am so awful to other kids, especially if they seem to have everything going for them – nice family, good marks, decent clothes. I know I shouldn't attack them just because they are lucky, but I can't seem to help it. Going to secondary school, I know there will be older bigger bullies than me so I want to stop acting this way."

Harry (12)

Well, Harry's reasons for trying to stop bullying aren't exactly charitable. He is really only worried about himself. Still, any reason to stop bullying is a good one. If you want to become a better person who doesn't bully others, try to:

- **apologise to your former victims if possible.** Do it privately and don't be too upset if they are still suspicious of you – they just need to get used to the 'new you'.

- **make amends or at least be pleasant to your former victims.** It might take them some time to trust you if you have hurt them in the past but don't be put off – keep on trying.

- **see if you can help new pupils in your year** – they may feel isolated. They won't know so much about your bullying past and might be glad of your friendship.

- **take up a sport** if you have lots of energy and find it difficult to sit still all day in school – your local leisure centre or football club will have details.

- **do voluntary work** – people outside school won't know that you have been a bully and won't be put off by your reputation.

- **visit a local youth club** – if you can make friends outside school, you won't feel so insecure and lonely.

- **take up any interests you may have or develop new ones.** Find out if there is a local club or society and join it.

- **take up judo or karate** if you are aggressive and find it hard not to lose your temper – these martial arts teach you how to control negative emotions and how to use your strength positively.

"*I get really mad if someone gives me grief. I don't think straight. Sometimes I hit people and get into fights.*"

Khalil (11)

- **learn how to control your anger and aggression.** See pages 72–76 in the assertiveness section. Angry, aggressive, unpredictable behaviour puts people off.

- **set yourself goals** (I won't bother Sally this morning, or I won't hassle Tony when I see him at lunch, or I'll try to be nice to Zeinab today.) It might sound stupid but it does work!

- **if you have a friend you trust, ask them to help.** Perhaps they could step in when they see you beginning to bully someone or be aggressive or violent.

- **talk to someone at school about the problem** and ask them if there is somewhere quiet you could go when your feelings are getting the better of you. Getting away can help you get control of yourself.

- **talk to your family and see if they can help.**

- **get counselling** if you cannot control your behaviour. The school or your doctor will have suggestions.

- **figure out a way to deal with your frustrations** – count to ten, leave the room, go for a walk or hit a punch bag if you feel angry or ready to explode.

- **think of how you would feel** if someone were treating you like you are treating your victim.

"I finally had enough of being a bully, but no one believed me when I said I wanted to change. The other kids would try to get me to fight and sometimes I did. But things are better now and I have a few friends who aren't afraid of me. It is hard to keep from being sarcastic because that's the way my mum talks to everyone. I've also got a boyfriend now, so things are looking up."

Elizabeth (14)

Don't get disheartened if you find yourself slipping back into bullying in spite of all your good resolutions. You won't become perfect overnight – changing behaviour takes time. After a setback, you have to pick yourself up and try again.

Getting rid of the bullying habit and learning how to make friends means you are taking positive steps to help yourself.

Adults who were bullies as children often end up with all sorts of problems – failed relationships, few friends, frequent job changes, even prison records – because they still think that being aggressive and unpleasant is the only way to behave. Save yourself future grief by stopping bullying now.

"I never had a feeling of power but I seemed to get satisfaction from beating up other kids. Inside I was scared. I thought nobody liked me. I had a big nose and I thought I was ugly. People used to tease me about it. I felt very insecure."

Mel (20)

"I never bullied anyone, but I did watch it happen. Now I feel guilty that I didn't help"

Bullying doesn't just harm the victim, it harms us all. I have talked with lots of kids who stood by and did nothing and they tell me that:

- they feel guilty about not stopping the bullying or at least going for help
- they feel worried that they might be the next victim
- they feel powerless and upset.

On a recent television programme, I was sitting next to a man who turned to me to confess his 20-year-old guilt at not having helped a classmate who was being bullied. "I think I was just as responsible for the bullying as the bully," he said. I agree that he was wrong not to have tried to help his classmate. So bullying harms us all – the victims, the bullies and the bystanders.

Remember

- Tell yourself you are a good person – one who doesn't bully and hurt others.
- You can change your behaviour if you really want to.
- Develop new interests and activities that will take you away from the chance to bully.
- Apologise to your victims, if possible.
- It won't be smooth sailing and you will make mistakes – that's OK. No one is perfect.

What if?

Nadine is friends with a group of kids who are bullies and she has bullied others. Although she feels badly about what she has done, she is scared to stop in case her friends turn against her. But she really does want to change.
Should she:

a) Continue to hang around with the same group, but try to get them to change?
b) Start finding new friends?
c) Start some new activities such as joining a sports club?
d) Tell her teachers and parents that she wants to turn over a new leaf?

It is not easy for anyone to change the behaviour of a group of people. It is difficult enough to change your own behaviour, especially if you have to go against your friends. So it may be best to try (b) and (c). People may be suspicious of Nadine at first, so starting a new activity will show them that she means what she says. New activities do help and will give her a different group of people to get to know. It won't be easy because her bully gang may turn on her – she should try not to make any comments about them. Perhaps she could just say she wants to move on and meet new people.

Tony, aged 12, was placed with a foster family because his mother was very ill and no one in the family could look after him.

"From the first time I walked into the house, the older boy bullied me. I guess he wasn't happy to have a foster brother and he made my life hell. He would hide my books, 'accidentally' spill something on my homework, trip me up and generally try to annoy me. Of course he was clever and never got caught. My foster mum couldn't understand why I seemed to be always hitting her son – she never saw him bullying me before I lashed out at him. I never hit him for nothing – only when he pushed and pushed me until I couldn't take any more. Eventually the family didn't want me any more, so I guess the bully won in the end. I got bullied at school, as well, so maybe it's something about me that is the problem."

By the time Tony contacted me, it was too late to fix the bullying problem at the foster home because he was now in another home. I think Tony should have told his foster mum, but maybe he didn't think she'd believe him. However, the bullying at school is still going on, so what do you think Tony should do about it:

a) Realise that he is the problem and that he deserves to be bullied?
b) Take a class in martial arts?
c) Try to tell a teacher, his social worker, a youth leader or someone at school?
d) Ring a helpline and talk it over?

I think Tony might try taking a course in martial arts — not to become the next Jackie Chan but to increase his self-confidence, and he should either tell someone or ring a helpline like ChildLine and talk over what he could do. He does not deserve the bullying and he should not put up with it.

CHAPTER FOUR

Self-assertiveness

These extracts are from letters that I received in one week from three 13-year-old students:

"I was bullied for three years. The bullying stopped when we moved to a new neighbourhood and school. I have friends now, but I am shy and sometimes I feel like people take advantage of me. I don't need counselling or anything like that, I just want to be able to say what I mean without feeling so embarrassed and wimpy all the time. Is there anything I can do?"

Diane (13)

"I used to be a bully. I still am sometimes, but hardly at all any more. The problem is when people don't respect me or listen to me, I get mad and push them around. My mum says I have to learn to control my temper and I am trying. She said to write to you and ask if you had any ideas."

Patrick (13)

"Thank you for writing to me. I tried several of your suggestions and am feeling a little more confident now. When Joyce [the bully] demanded that I give her my homework to copy, I took a deep breath, looked her in the eye and said NO in a loud voice. She couldn't believe it and neither could I. She tried a couple more times, but I stood my ground. I helped my friend do the same and now Joyce leaves us both alone. Thank you."

Sheila (13)

Diane is **passive**. She has much in common with other children who have been bullied – she lacks confidence and feels she isn't very assertive.

Patrick is **aggressive**. He acts before he thinks and lashes out at people if he doesn't get his own way. He doesn't know how to get what he wants in a nice way.

Sheila is becoming **assertive**. She is learning how to stand up for herself without hurting other people. She is also helping her friend, so the two of them can be strong together.

If you are a victim of bullying or if you bully other people, practising some basic self-assertiveness skills can help you feel better about yourself. Self-assertiveness training can also teach you different ways of responding to difficult or upsetting situations.

Patrick, Sheila and Diane show the three ways you can respond to people:

- passive
- aggressive
- assertive

Passive people behave as if other people's rights matter more than their own.
Aggressive people behave as if their own rights matter more than those of others.
Assertive people respect themselves and others equally.

Roughly, victims tend to be passive and bullies tend to be aggressive. *You can change your behaviour from passive or aggressive to become assertive. Try some of the suggestions below. Practise by yourself, looking into a mirror perhaps, or with a friend or parent.*

Thoughts

"How can I stop thinking such bad things about myself? My brother says I am my own worst enemy."

Joe (12)

The thoughts we have about ourselves can help or hurt the way we respond to others.

Often we put ourselves down:
- "No one will like me."
- "I am hopeless at this."
- "I'll never get it right."

We can change this and say helpful things to ourselves instead:
- "I have the right to ask for what I want."
- "I did OK. It wasn't perfect but it was OK."
- "I am a good person."

Making requests

"The bullying has made me so self-conscious that I can't even ask my own sister to turn down her music because I am afraid she'll yell at me. Is there something I can do about this? I can't go the rest of my life not saying anything."

Rowena (13)

Rowena blushes and stammers whenever she needs to make a request of anyone, including her teachers, her family and her friends. Bullying can affect people this way. So there are three basic rules you can remember if you want to overcome this problem:

1. **Be clear about what you want.**
2. **Make your request short** (for example, "That is my pencil. I would like it back please.").
3. **Plan and practise** (even if you just go over the request in your own mind).

You have to decide what you are going to say and then stick to it. ("That is my pencil. I want it back.") Don't allow yourself to be side-tracked away from the main issue: it is your pencil and you want it back.

If the person you are talking to is trying to be difficult, just quietly keep repeating your request. Take a deep breath and plant your feet firmly on the ground. Then try saying whatever your request is. For example, "Please stop that". A word of warning – it is no good asking repeatedly for a million pounds or a Ferrari!

Here are some suggestions as to what you could say in difficult situations:

- I want to turn off the television.
- I don't want to walk home that way – let's go a different way.
- I'm not going into that shop.
- Those shoes do not fit, please bring me a different size.
- That dog frightens me – I don't want to go near it.
- I will not give you my homework to copy.
- I would like you to move please.
- I am listening to that music – please don't change it.
- That is my book – please give it to me.
- Please return my jacket now.
- I don't want to loan you my watch.

Responses to bully demands

"The girl who bullies me doesn't hit me or anything like that, but she makes me give her things like money or my lunch. I wish I could think of something to say. Has anyone tried anything that worked?"

Anna (10)

When a bully makes a demand, it is sometimes difficult to know what to say. It is a good idea to practise some responses to specific demands and to come up with your own creative ideas. Warning – don't try responses that will make things worse, like "you're so stupid you couldn't even *copy* my homework" or similar clever comments. I know you can think of lots like that! The trouble is, then you are being aggressive instead of assertive and you might get into trouble.

Try some ideas like these:

"Got any sweets on you?"

"Yes, but they're horrible. Anyway, I licked them."

"Sorry, they're all gone."

I've only licked a few but I can't remember which ones...

SWEETS

"Lend us your homework."

> "OK, but the teacher has already seen it – I talked to him this morning."
>
> "No, I've not finished it myself."

"Lend us your dinner money."

> "Go ahead and have it all, but I'll have to explain to the teacher why I'm so hungry."
>
> "No, borrow it from the teacher, why don't you?"

"We'll be waiting for you after school (at the toilets etc.)."

> "Fine, should we arrange it with the teacher/Head?"
>
> "I'd like to be there, but I've got a more important appointment."

"You've got my book in your bag – I need to look inside it."

> "Let's get someone to help then – how about the teacher?"
>
> "Your book is not in my bag. Shall we go to the Head and sort it out?"

"I'm still waiting for you to give me that CD."

> "It's a shame, but my sister lost it."
>
> "Did you say you wanted to go to the shop and buy a CD? Try Virgin, I think they have it."
>
> "The teacher has it and would love to talk to you about it."

Saying no

"I think I am getting better now because the bully was excluded from school and the other kids are starting to be human again. The problem is that I try to please everyone when sometimes I just want to say no. Can you send me some ideas about what to do?"

Iain (13)

Everyone should learn to say NO and to stick to it. There might be times when someone asks you to shoplift or cheat in an exam or take drugs or whatever and you will want to say no and get away. It helps if you think about it in advance.

Just remember that you have the right to say no. It is not selfish to say no and there are times when you should say no.

Here are some tips that work:

- **Decide what you are going to say and stick to it.** Be kind but firm "No. I am sorry that you don't have a pencil but I don't want to lend you my pencil".

- **Keep your body assertive**, feet firmly on the ground and shoulders and head held high. Don't smile, and keep good eye-contact. The other person will know from the way you are speaking and standing that you are serious.

TOWER HAMLETS COLLEGE
Learning Centre
Poplar High Street
LONDON
E14 0AF

- **Practise looking people in the eye,** if it is difficult for you. Do this with friends and family or a mirror.

- **When you say NO, say it firmly.**

- **Don't get side–tracked into apologising** for your decision or justifying it. Don't make excuses.

- **Listen to your body and to your feelings:** what do you really want to say? What do you really want to do?

- **Try not to get caught up in arguments** and don't become angry or upset if you don't get your own way.

- **If you don't want to do something, don't give in to pressure.** Be firm. Remember, we have the right to say NO.

- **If you are not sure and somebody is pushing you for an answer,** say "I need more time to decide" or "I need more information".

- **Offer an alternative:** "No, I don't want to play football. Let's go for a walk instead."

When we say no to someone, we are only refusing the request. We are not rejecting the person.

Saying no responses

- No, I don't want to leave right now. But you can go – I'll catch up later.
- No, you cannot borrow my gym clothes – sorry.
- No, I don't like that.
- No, there is no way I can do that.
- No, leave me alone, please. I don't want to do that now.
- No, it is my book and I need it. Maybe I can help you find one.

- No, it just isn't possible for me to go with you. I have too much work to do.
- No, you cannot have my chocolate – anyway I've licked it.
- No, I cannot loan you any money. I've only got enough for the bus and if I don't come home on it my mother will ring the Head.

Shouting no

This is different from firmly saying NO. This is a loud, deep, great shout to use if you are in trouble or danger and need to get help fast. If you are frightened for your safety, shout as loud as you possibly can. Make it sound like a foghorn, not a high squeaky noise like a mouse. Shout from your stomach, not your throat. The object is to attract as much attention as possible and to scare off the person who is trying to hurt you.

How to deal with taunts and insults

"It's hard to take when people are insulting you and you don't deserve it. The insults are worse than the punches somehow. I wish I could just ignore what the bully says, but I don't know how."

James (11)

James has the same problem as lots of people. If someone insults us and we insult them back, then things can get out of hand. Both bullies and victims then end up spending all their time thinking up new and more horrible insults! It isn't fair that someone insults you, but there are ways to just let it go by you until the person gets tired of trying to get you to respond.

We can 'fog'. What are you talking about, I hear you say. Think of how banks of fog swallow up everything you can see and deaden sounds. Being in a fog bank is eerie, but also protective – no one can see you or get at you. So when other people make hurtful remarks we don't have to argue or become upset; we can protect ourselves with 'fog' and swallow up what they say.

You can either say nothing and let the insult be swallowed by the fog or you can say something short and bland like:

- "That's what you think"
- "You could be right"
- "It's possible"
- "Really?"

The trick is not to take the insult personally, if you can.

Relaxing

"When I get home from school I am so wound up that my body feels like it is tied up in knots. I can't concentrate on doing my homework and my head throbs. Is there something I can do?"

Lee (12)

If you are tense and unhappy, you may find it very hard to relax. But relaxing is good for you – it helps you start thinking more clearly and keep your body healthy.

Try the following simple exercise when you are alone:

- Lie on the floor.
- Tense all your muscles until they feel really rigid.
- Slowly relax your muscles, starting with your toes and gradually working up to your head. At the end you should be floppy like a rag doll.

Try this before you go to bed at night if you are having trouble sleeping.

Posture

"The only way I could get away from the bullying was by keeping my head down and my eyes to the ground. Otherwise, the bullies said things like "Who you looking at" or "I don't like the way you're staring at me" even though I wasn't trying to cause trouble. My mum says my posture is terrible. What can I do?"

Rosalie (14)

If you have poor posture and tend to creep about with your head down and shoulders slumped, you need to learn how to stand up straight, how to walk confidently and how to make eye-contact. It isn't easy to get over the habit of bending over. When I was young, my grandmother suggested that we all walk around with books on our heads (at home!). My sister and I did and it helped, so that is one thing you can do. Practise in front of a mirror.

It might help if you observe how other people behave. Watch and note how they make eye contact. Look at the way people stand and the way they walk. Listen to their tone of voice and to the way they say things. Which people seem to be the most confident? I suspect you will find that people who look others in the eye and stand tall with their heads held high seem to be the most confident.

When you are watching these people (don't stare at them or they will wonder what your problem is) think about what is passive, what is aggressive and what is assertive behaviour.

Then go home and practise walking tall, standing straight and looking assertive even if you don't feel that way inside. Eventually you will.

Dealing with anger

"When I get angry, I can't control myself. I end up
bullying people and then get into trouble myself. I want to
learn to control my temper, but it seems impossible.
My teacher says that I will end up being kicked out of
school if I don't stop."

Kevin (13)

If you lose your temper or become violent and
aggressive easily, you need to practise controlling
these feelings. It is not necessarily wrong to get angry
but it is wrong to take out your anger on others.
It might help to think about why people get angry.
I asked a group of 12-year-olds and they said they
thought people get angry because:

> they don't get what they want
> they are frustrated
> they cannot do their school work
> they are hurt and afraid to show it
> they feel hard done by
> they feel frightened or stupid
> they are being abused and can't tell someone
> they are used to getting their own way.

I don't know why Kevin gets angry, but it is important
that he thinks about it so he can start to control it.
More about that in a minute.

It is also important that Kevin knows that it is
sometimes all right to be angry. The same group of
12-year-olds said that they thought being angry
was OK:

if something is unfair
if someone is being harmed
if someone is being bullied
if someone is being called racist names
if people have been abused.

They also said that it anger isn't acceptable:

if it is used to deliberately hurt someone
if is used unfairly
if it is used to gain power over someone
if it makes you feel sick
if it is turned against yourself.

So what can Kevin do?

- **learn to recognise the signs** that he is about to 'explode' and work out what to do instead of exploding. He could dig his nails into the palm of his hand or grit his teeth or tell himself to calm down.

- **get away** from the situation or the person that is making him angry – *this is not 'running away'*. This is just the best way of keeping himself and others from getting hurt either through a fight or through arguments and name-calling.

- **take several deep breaths** and count to ten

If the situation needs to be sorted out and Kevin must stay and deal with it, then he should:

- **state the reasons** for his anger calmly and be specific:

"I'm angry because you didn't meet me at the
cinema like you promised."
"I am angry that you took that book away
from me."
"I am angry that you stepped on my toe."

Kevin may find that the other person didn't know
what he or she had done. They may apologise and
that will be the end of it. If this doesn't happen, then
he can:

- **State what he would like to happen** to remedy
  the situation: "You owe me an apology" or
  "I expect you to replace the CD you lost".

The next steps are to:

- **Listen** to what the other person says without
  interrupting.

- **Stick to the problem** – don't bring up all the sins
  of the past, or say "You're always doing that".

- **Try not to use blame in a vague way** – it's better to explain "It makes me angry when you take my video game without asking", than say "You're a terrible person for taking my game and I hate you".

If Kevin cannot get the other person to be reasonable, then he may find his anger rising. The best thing to do then is to leave and **get help** from an adult to sort it out.

One other suggestion, if Kevin finds he is still angry, is to **exercise**. It helps you let off steam – go for a walk or play football or get on your bicycle, for example.

If you get angry, if might help to fill out your own questionnaire to help you think about what triggers your anger and what you can do about it. On a separate piece of paper, finish off the following sentences:

I feel angry when...
I wish I could say to someone I feel angry with...
There are times when I feel like...
Anger is good when...
Anger is bad when...
I wish that...would not be angry with me.
If I tell someone I am angry, they will...
The way I express my anger is...
When I get angry I...
I think the most positive way to deal with being angry is...
Next time I feel angry I will...

Remember

- You have the right to be assertive.
- You have a responsibility to respect the rights of others.
- When you make a request, make it clearly and firmly.
- You may have to pretend a lot at first and act in a way you don't really feel. But eventually the 'acting' will cease and you will be more assertive than you thought possible!
- You can learn to control your anger and learn to be assertive in a nice way.

What if?

John has been being bullied at school for two years. He has had his clothes ripped and his money stolen and he is kicked and punched nearly every day. Recently, John finally plucked up enough courage to tell his dad. Instead of sympathising, his dad told him "don't be a wimp – the only way to handle a bully is to just go and punch him in the nose." John is terrified of doing this and suspects that he will end up worse off in a fight. Should he:

a) Follow that advice?
b) Do nothing?
c) Take up martial arts, then follow the advice?
d) Talk to someone else?

John's dad is like a lot of other people who tell kids to just punch the bully. Of course, sometimes it does work and the bullying stops. But it can make things much worse. The problem is that not only could John get hurt more than he is now, but he might also get in trouble for punching someone. Taking a martial arts class (c) is a good idea to help him build up his confidence – not to give him ways of beating up people. He should take it for himself. What he might find is that the bullying stops because the classes in self-defence help him so he no longer thinks of himself as a victim and nor does the bully. Also, John needs to find another adult (d) to talk to!

Ben is walking into the lunch room when someone yells across the room, "Here comes fat boy – make way for the whale". Ben wishes he could drop through the floor. How should he respond?

   a)   Ignore the comment?
   b)   Yell back?
   c)   Report it to his teacher or a trusted adult?

He can either (a) ignore it (if it is the first time and Ben can pretend it didn't bother him) or tell someone (c) if it really bothers him or if the person calling names has done it before to him or to other kids. Some people might think that it is a good idea to yell back, but that probably wouldn't solve anything. You would be seen as a stronger person if you could just hold your head high and ignore the idiot that shouted.

CHAPTER FIVE

Making Friends

Learning to like yourself

Before you can make friends with other people, you need to make friends with yourself.

"The bullying has stopped, but I still feel so useless. What can I do to help myself?"

John (14)

If you have been bullied for a long time, you might start to believe what the bully says – that you are ugly and awful and that no one will ever like you. *This is not true: this is 'victim-think'.*

One way to stop being a victim is to stop thinking like a victim.

To help you start feeling better about yourself, about the way you look and about the way you are, try doing some mental exercises to build up your self-confidence. It's not as stupid as it sounds – after all, a body-builder does physical exercises to build up muscles.

What you can do to feel better about yourself

- **make a list of all the good things you can think of about yourself**. Don't say there aren't any! Everyone has talents so think about what you do best. The next time you feel down, think about the good things on your list. When people say nice things about you or praise you, *write them down*. A diary doesn't just have to record the bad things that happen to you.

- **learn to talk to yourself in a positive way**. Instead of saying "I am hopeless at Maths" say something like "Maths is the pits but at least I can work my calculator." Or instead of "I am so ugly no one will ever like me" say "I may not look like a super model but who wants to look like one anyway? I've got a brilliant sense of humour!".

- **if you have a particular interest, develop your skill:** whatever it is, find out if there are local courses available or if there is a club or society you can join.

- **do some voluntary work.** Charities need volunteers and helping other people is a good way to forget about your problems. I know several 10 to 14-year-olds who help out in Soup Kitchens. The Library or Citizens Advice Bureau will have details of local groups. Think about doing a First Aid course with St John's Ambulance or the Red Cross.

- **if you are interested in a particular cause,** whether it's politics, the environment, or animal rights, find out about joining a group. They will welcome supporters. Ask at your local library.

- **join a Youth Club, religious group or other organisation.** If you have interests outside school and meet more people, you will realise how much you have to offer and how narrow-minded and limited bullies are.

- **think about going to martial arts or self-defence classes** – not to turn into Rambo, but to increase your self-confidence. Learning how to defend yourself makes you feel less helpless – less like a victim. Your local leisure centre or youth club will have details.

- **practise the assertiveness tips in chapter four** – they really can help you to feel more confident. See if there are any assertiveness training classes held locally.

It takes time to get over bullying. Once the bullying stops, many victims say that they don't feel brilliant immediately. But you **will** feel better eventually. Some adults who were bullied as kids have told us that they think the bullying made them stronger inside – they became determined to do well to prove how wrong the bullies were.

"I was bullied the whole time I was at school. Sometimes I felt so bad, I wished I could die. Now I think that getting through it has given me a lot of strength – I feel determined to do well just to show all the other kids what I'm really like. I know that two of the blokes who bullied me have been inside twice – they've already messed up their lives. That's not going to happen to me."

Liam (19)

Making friends with other people

"I want to make friends, but I don't know how. In my last school I was bullied and kicked around and didn't have any friends. The kids at this school seem to be OK, but I just know I'll do something wrong. Help."

Richard (11)

F unny, isn't it, that we think everyone knows how to make friends. A lot of people don't and I have even found that some bullies end up bullying because they don't know what to do either. Then they get stuck with the label of bully and don't know how to change.

Perhaps the best way to think about making friends is to decide what makes a friend. I asked a group of 13-year-olds to come up with a list of what they liked about their friends. They said that good friends:

* show an interest in what people do
* are good at giving compliments without going overboard
* go around with a pleasant expression on their face
* laugh at people's jokes
* are kind
* ask, not demand, to join in
* offer to help others with work or carry things
* invite people to do something
* hang around places where other students are
* are welcoming to new students
* are good at thinking of something interesting to do

- are willing to share
- are humorous and tell jokes
- are fair
- are good at organising games or activities

I then asked the group to think about ways NOT to make friends. They thought that doing the following would turn people off:

- being bossy
- telling others how to behave
- telling others they are doing things wrong
- talking about yourself all the time
- being mean
- talking about other people behind their back
- being negative and sarcastic
- being too intense or serious all the time
- bragging
- moaning all the time
- being a bully
- claiming credit for something you didn't do
- lying or cheating

Looking at what the students said, let's answer Richard's question.

I think that Richard's problems stem from the time he was bullied. He has lost the confidence to make and keep friends. Not having friends is very difficult. You can imagine the lonely feelings when you have no one to sit with at lunch or go to places with on the weekends.

Decide on a plan

Think about your skills

The first thing Richard needs to do is to work on his 'people skills'. If he would like to make new friends, he can make sure he:

- has good eye contact. Looking in a pleasant way at people shows you are interested in them.

- listens to what the other person says. Listening is an important skill. Everyone likes other people to pay attention to what they say – it makes them feel good.

- looks friendly. No one wants to be around someone who scowls and emits unfriendly signals. Sometimes you may need to act friendly, even if you don't feel that way. You may have to be an actor and pretend.

- practises his opening lines when approaching another person. For example, "What did you think of the English test?"

Think about how many friends you want

Richard doesn't have to find hundreds of new friends, one or two will do fine. Some people seem to have thousands of friends; others just a few.

"I like having lots of friends around me and always going somewhere and doing something fun."

Hamish (10)

As far as Hamish is concerned, the more the merrier and he isn't happy unless there is action most of the time.

"I've only ever had one or two close friends. I like being on my own or doing something with Gareth or Dai."

Frank (12)

Frank has always had a few close friends and likes to get together to talk or go to the cinema or play on the computer or just go for walks in the woods.

Even if you decide in the end that you want lots of friends, it is best to start with finding one or two. It is less stressful and more likely to succeed.

Think about what you would like in a friend

So Richard should think about what he would like in a friend and then he can look around and see who he might approach. Having talked to him about his interests, I suspect his ideal friend:

- would be nice to him and not bully him

- would enjoy music, computer games and camping or outdoor type activities like riding bikes

- would be his friend at lunch and break times

- would like to come over to his flat

- would be kind and thoughtful

- would not be too loud or boisterous

- likes to laugh

Think about who you want to approach

Richard should choose someone who has been friendly. It is probably a good idea to try to make friends with someone who may not be the 'most popular' kid, but someone who seems nice and who may want to make more friends, as well. It might be that he puts only one or two names on his mental list.

Think about starting small

You don't need to rush up to someone and say "can you come over to my flat on Saturday and we'll go swimming and have a picnic and . . ." The other person might be quite put off. Friendships take time. The first step is to start the conversation. This can be scary. Adults I know say that any intelligent thought they've ever had banishes and they become blithering idiots when beginning a conversation with someone they hardly know.

What Richard needs is a practised phrase or two he can use that slips out easily and gets him over that first hurdle. How about something like:

- "Did you see the programme last night about . . .? What did you think of it?" Since most people watch television, this could be a common starting point.

- "What did you think about the story we had to read for homework (or in class)?"

- "I liked your drawing. What kinds of things do you like to draw?"

- "What did you do over the holiday (or weekend)?"

- "Would you like to go over there and play that game – or do you have any other suggestions?"

- "Would it be OK if I sat here next to you?"

Again this is something you could practise. I certainly recommend that Richard practise his opening lines either with a family member or in the mirror or to the wall, if necessary.

Think about what you and your friends could do

After he has started talking to kids at school, Richard might want to invite them over or arrange to do something after school.

He needs to think of things he and his friends could do, like going cycling or going to the cinema. He could make a list of possibilities and find out how to organise something. Remember that organising things was on the first list made up by the 13-year-olds earlier in this chapter.

Maybe there is a swimming pool near you or an ice rink. It is also fun to do things like play board games like Monopoly and have snacks to eat. You might rent a DVD or take the dog for a walk in the park. Or try cooking a pizza, if your parents agree. Or have an ice-cream party where everyone makes their own concoctions and probably gets sick from eating too much!

Think about changing your behaviour

Richard had no undesirable behaviour to change, unless you count his sensitivity. I wouldn't call that bad behaviour – just a result of having been bullied before. He had to be careful not to think everyone was trying to get at him. It wasn't easy for Richard, but he found that he made more friends if he shrugged things off and didn't react to silly little things that bothered him. For example, the boys might come up and say "hello, freak" to each other. They didn't really mean anything by it, but you can see if you were bullied that this would seem to be aimed at you personally. It wasn't – they all called each other that. Yes, it was a stupid remark, but not worth making a big deal about or taking personally.

Some people have to change their habits if they want to make friends. Things like

- having a quick temper
- being bossy or refusing to share
- farting
- burping

- picking your nose or spitting
- being smelly
- having disgustingly dirty hair or fingernails

Don't be surprised if people avoid you if you don't take care of yourself!

Realise that it doesn't always work out

Friendships won't always go according to plan. You may try to be friends with someone, but it just doesn't work out for reasons you can't do anything about. It could just be that you can't find anything in common. It might be that you used to be friends but now enjoy doing completely different things. Or a friend may have personal problems and just want to be left alone for a while.

Friends also may decide to do something which you do not want to do like shoplift, bully someone, throw things at cars or take drugs. Keep in mind that real friends do not force people to do things that are harmful to themselves or to others. So if a friend says "let's steal from the store and if you don't I won't be your friend anymore" or "if you don't join in bullying that kid, then our friendship is over", then the friendship wasn't 'worth spit'.

Some friendships come and go. Some will last a lifetime, others only a day. If you've tried your best, perhaps it just wasn't meant to be, as my grandmother used to say.

Develop new skills, activities, interests

You can increase the number of people you can be friends with by developing your skills and interests. If you like sports, find out about Saturday sports clubs or after school lessons. Look into swimming, dance, tennis and gymnastics classes. Check out the local Scouts and Girl Guides, acting or martial arts classes. See if you can take music lessons, or learn to play the guitar. Not only will these things increase your self-confidence, they will give you a whole new group of people from which to find friends.

Keeping your friends

"Susan and Anne used to both be my friends. We have known each other for five years, ever since starting school. This year they became friends with Cara and now they all ignore me and whisper about me. I feel so awful."

Lynn (10)

Whatever you do, please don't throw away old friends when you make new ones. Fickle friends break many a heart. Most of the best friends I have are those I have known for over thirty years, and some are school friends. Perhaps that's because they haven't been around me much!

By the way, Richard rang me a few weeks ago to tell me how things were going. He now has a group of four friends and they do most things together. He is still a bit sensitive, but he hides it well. Richard tries to be especially nice to new kids because he remembers what it was like to be one. His advice is to not sit back and let the bullies win. Get out there and make friends.

Remember

- smile, be pleasant and say hi to people. We are all more attracted to nice people.
- make the first move. Reach out and don't always wait for someone else to say hello or ask you to do something.
- learn to be a good listener. Everyone likes to be listened to and it is one of the things people value most in a friend.

- don't expect everyone to be just like you. It is better to have friends who have their own ideas and opinions. It would be boring if we all thought and acted the same.

- ask lots of questions. A good way to let other people know you are interested in them is to ask about what they like and what they think.

- don't moan all the time. If you only use your friends to talk about your problems, they will get tired of hearing constant tales of woe. Talk about good things, as well.

- beware of false friends. Sometimes we stay with friends because there is no one else around. Watch out for 'friends' who try to make you do things you don't want to do or which you know are wrong.

- don't bug people – if they don't want to be friends, move on to someone else. Not all friendships work out.

What if?

Sean has just become friends with a group of kids at school. He is thrilled to be in the group and for several weeks everything goes well. Then one day the whole group decides that they are going to play truant. They tell Sean that either he goes with them or they will exclude him from now on. "If you want to be friends with us, you have to be loyal. If we skip school, so do you." Sean desperately wants to remain friends, but he doesn't want to play truant. What should he do?

a) Go along with them just this once?
b) Stay in school?
c) Tell the teacher that the group is playing truant?
d) Tell if they bully him?

Sean is in a real dilemma because he wants to be in this group, but they aren't really his friends if they are demanding that he does something against his better judgement. Threatening to exclude him is cruel. What will they ask next? Sean shouldn't go (b)! If they start bullying him then he should tell someone about the bullying (d). If they skip school but don't bully him or give him grief, then let them get caught on their own.

Marion has been best friends with three other girls in her class for two years but things have started to go wrong. For some reason her friends have turned on her and they've begun to ignore her. They won't sit with her at lunch because they say she is too boring and stupid to spend time with. Marion's feelings are very hurt and she is quite miserable. Should she:

a) Tell her parents?
b) Do nothing?
c) Ring one member of the group and ask them why they are doing this?
d) Try to find a new group?

Marion could certainly talk to her parents (a) and try to get one or two members of the group on their own (c) to see if she can stop their behaviour. It sometimes works to have the parents, if they are friends, talk to each other. Marion could also try to find a new group (d) because this group may not be worth having as friends if they are so cruel to her.

CHAPTER SIX

Exercises that help

About yourself questionnaire

This is a private exercise to help you start thinking of some good things about yourself. If you have been bullied or have been a bully, you may want to get rid of those bad images of yourself.

Take a separate piece of paper and write your answers down. Even if you can't think of lots of things, try to come up with at least one. Then tomorrow or the next day or next week, add things. Perhaps you could show your answers to a parent or a teacher you trust and see if they can help you think of more things. Be careful about sharing them with friends in case they decide to talk about it to others.

1.   *What are your favourite television programmes?*

2.   *What are your favourite sports, bands, hobbies, activities?*

3.   *Name one thing you are proud of doing.*

4.   *Name five good things about yourself.*

5.   *List five words that best describe you.*

6.   *List five words that describe your family.*

7.   *What do you like to do most?*

8.   *What do you like to do least?*

9.   *Who would you like as a friend?*

     Why?

10. *Who would you most like to be like?*

     Why?

11. *What is it about friends that you most value?*

12. *What is it that makes people like you?*

13. *List five things you would like to have done by the time you are 21.*

14. *List five things you would like to have done by the time you are 100.*

15. *What do you like/dislike about school?*

16. *How would you change school if you had a magic wand?*

17. *How would you change yourself if you had a magic wand?*

Your thoughts

This exercise can help you to think about yourself and what you value. Some of the answers might make you think about things you are good at or find funny. It is good to laugh and stop thinking all the time about bullying. It is fun to share this with someone because it gives you something to talk about and a way to get to know someone else. You don't have to write everything down, you could take turns with friends at giving the answer out loud.

1. What have you done that makes you most happy?

2. Do you like your name? Would you change it? To what?

3. What is the best thing that has ever happened to you?

4. What is the weirdest thing that has ever happened to you?

5. What is the silliest thing you have ever done?

6. What is the funniest thing that has ever happened to you?

7. What person do you most admire? Why?

8. What qualities do you look for in a friend?

9. What is your best quality?

10. What is the most important thing in your life?

11. What one thing would you change about yourself?

12. What one thing would you change about school?

13. What do you hate doing most in the whole world?

14. What do you like doing most in the whole world?

15. If you could be anyone in the whole world, who would you be and why?

I am proud that

Think about some things that make you feel proud. It is good to feel proud. I bet your parents can add to the list, if you feel like sharing it with them.

I am proud that:

1. My family is...

2. I tried very hard to...

3. I did well in...

4. I did not...

5. I am good at...

6. I helped...

7. I always ...

8. I have improved at...

9. I will become...

10. My ambition is to...

No matter what

If someone is calling you names and for some reason you can't get away, this is a way to go inside your head and tune out what the other person is saying. Repeat silently to yourself:

'No matter what you say, I'm a good person'.

Think loudly and with feeling:

'NO MATTER WHAT YOU SAY, I'M A GOOD PERSON'.

While you are saying this to yourself, keep your body straight with your shoulders back. If you feel confident enough, stare at the bully and just keep thinking 'I'm a good person'.

You may not even believe it, but eventually you will because you are a good person and no one should be calling you names! Practise at home by thinking of what people have said that has bothered you.

Anita, age 11, came up with this list:

- You're stupid
- You look funny in those glasses
- Guess you forgot to put on your face today
- Nice dress too bad about the body
- Ugly
- Think you're smart?

Anita looked at all these terrible comments and decided to practise ignoring them. Her mother helped by pretending to be the bully and repeating the words the bully used. Every time a negative comment was made, Anita said out loud "I'm a good person, no matter what you say". She became more and more assertive and really began to believe what was true – *she was a good person*, no matter what the bully said. Finally she felt confident enough to look the bully in the eye and think in her own mind "I'm a good person" whenever the bully bothered her. Because Anita felt good about herself, the bully got no reaction, got bored and stopped picking on her. Anita's self-confidence increased so much that when she found out the bully had found another victim, Gaby, she offered to help the girl and they went together to tell the teacher. The bullying stopped altogether and Anita and Gaby became good friends.

Plan of action

If you are caught up in bullying, either as a victim or a bully, work out a plan to help yourself.

Ask yourself a few questions:

1 Am I happy with the way things are going? If not, what can I do to change things?

2 Am I doing something to make myself or others unhappy? If so, it is my responsibility to change.

3 What can I do differently?

4 What will happen if I continue as I am? What choices do I have (make a list)? What one thing can I work on today, this week, this year?

5 Plan it out – what will I do when I see the person I am bullying?

6 What will I do if I see the person who is bullying me?

7 Should I be changing anything I am doing? If so, how?

8 What will be my goal for the day or week or term?

"I was a bully, but I really didn't like myself much. I got into so much trouble that it finally came to either I was going to be excluded from school or I had to change. That's when I woke up to what I was doing."

Nicholas, 13

Nicholas's goal was to stop bullying two boys he had tormented for six months. He worked out the following plan with me:

1 I will not go to where I know Stan or Chu (his victims) are.

2 If we come face to face I will not say anything and will just walk away.

3 I won't bother people or act stupidly during break-time.

4 I won't go home until Stan and Chu have had lots of time to get home.

5 I will try to smile when I see Stan and Chu instead of making faces at them.

6 I won't allow Ross (another bully) to wind me up.

7 If Ross tries to get me to be a bully again, I will say "I'm not interested" and walk away.

It wasn't easy for Nicholas to change his behaviour and he did slip once or twice, but the plan worked for him. If you are being bullied, work out a plan like this for yourself. It helps to write it down and think about it in advance.

After a week or so, think about how the plan is working:

• How did you feel?
• What else could you have done?
• Did what you do help the situation or make it worse?
• What will you try next?
• Can you name one thing that changed for the better?
• What did you learn about yourself?
• What is your goal now?

Think of your goal and keep trying. Get help from someone you trust – everyone needs support.

So, let's end on the good news and the bad news. The bad news is that bullying is still going on in some places and some people still think it doesn't matter. Some schools seem to turn a blind eye to bullying.

If you are in a school like that explain to your parents just how bad it is, or contact one of the numbers at the back of this book.

The good news is that lots of people are speaking out now against bullying and trying to help kids who are being bullied. There are great schools where the teachers stop bullying in its tracks. You may be lucky enough to be in such a school – there are more and more of them around. And another piece of good news is that there's a lot that you can do to put an end to the bullying if you believe in yourself.

Just remember, if you or a friend are being bullied or if you are a bully and you want to stop, tell someone and keep telling until someone does something to help. Don't put up with bullying. After all, it isn't clever to be a bully and no one deserves to be bullied – ever!

Books about bullying

You may want to read other books about bullying and helping yourself. Here are a few that might interest you. See if you can get them from your library or check with your local book shop.

BULLIES, BIGMOUTHS AND SO CALLED FRIENDS
by Jenny Alexander (Hodder)

THE TRIAL OF ANNA COTMAN
by Vivien Alcock (Mammoth)

CAT'S EYE
by Margaret Atwood (Virago Press)

THE CHOCOLATE WAR
by Robert Cormier (Puffin)

LORD OF THE FLIES
by William Golding (Faber & Faber)

CHICKEN
by Alan Gibbons (Orion Children's Books)

WHOSE SIDE ARE YOU ON?
by Alan Gibbons (Orion Children's Books)

THE FISH FLY LOW
by Steve May (Methuen)

SECRET FRIENDS
by Elizabeth Laird (Hodder Children's Books)

THE BULLYBUSTER'S JOKE BOOK
by John Byrne (Red Fox)

THE PRESENT TAKERS
by Aidan Chambers (Red Fox)

RHYME STEW
by Roald Dahl (Jonathan Cape)

WILLOW STREET KIDS BEAT THE BULLIES
by Michele Elliott (MacMillan Children's Books)

WILLOW STREET KIDS BE SMART, STAY SAFE
by Michele Elliott (MacMillan Children's Books)

A KESTREL FOR A KNAVE
by Barry Hines (Penguin Books)

TOM BROWN'S SCHOOLDAYS
by Thomas Hughes (Penguin Books)

TO KILL A MOCKINGBIRD
by Harper Lee (Pan Books)

BULLIES
by Ed Wicke (Kingsway)

THE BULLY
by Jan Needle (Puffin Books)

Resources

If you cannot talk to someone close to you like a parent, teacher, school nurse or your doctor, then try contacting some of these organisations which are set up to help.

The numbers are free if they start with 0800. Remember, some calls will show up on your parents' telephone bill, but these are all confidential lines – the people on the other end won't tell anyone about what you say. *ChildLine* and the *Samaritans* <u>won't</u> show up on the bill.

Counselling advice and information

Kidscape
Tel: 08451 205 204
www.kidscape.org.uk

Kidscape has lots of useful information about bullying on its website, for both young people and parents. Kidscape also produces free booklets and leaflets about bullying and safety. To get a copy, send a large self addressed stamped envelope with 6 stamps to:

Kidscape
2 Grosvenor Gardens
London SW1W 0DH

The telephone line (a local rate number) is for parents to talk about how to help their children who are either being bullied or who are bullies. The line is open Monday to Friday 10 am to 4 pm.

ChildLine
Tel: 0800 1111
www.childline.org.uk

Children who are deaf or find using a regular phone difficult should use the textphone service on 0800 400 222. The line is open 9.30 am to 9.30 pm weekdays and 9.30 am to 8 pm weekends.

NSPCC
Tel: 0808 800 5000
www.nspc.org.uk

Their confidential online advice for 12–16 year olds can be found at www.there4me.com

Samaritans
Tel: 08457 909090
www.samaritans.org

A 24-hour confidential helpline for anyone with

problems. Some areas of the country also have drop-in centres

Young Minds
Tel: 0800 018 2138
www.youngminds.org.uk

A free and confidential telephone service providing information and advice for any adult with concerns about the mental health of a child or young person. The line is open on Monday and Friday 10 am to 1 pm, and on Tuesday, Wednesday and Thursday 1 to 4 pm, and Wednesday evenings from 6 to 8pm.

Young Minds produce leaflets and booklets to help young peopleand parents understand what to do when a young person feels troubled and where to find help.

Alcoholism

Al-Anon and Alateen
Tel: 020 7403 0888
www.al-anon.uk.org.uk
Email: nonuk@aol.com
The helpline operates from 10 am to 10 pm everyday.

Al-Anon is a network of self-help groups offering understanding and support for families and friends of problem drinkers.

Alateen is for young people aged 12 to 20 who have been affected by someone else's drinking, usually that of a parent.

Anorexia/bulimia/other eating disorders

Eating Disorders Association (EDA)
Tel: 08456 347650
www.edauk.com
Email: talkback@eda.uk.com

A helpline for 18-year-olds and under. The line is open
4 to 6.30 pm Monday to Friday and 1 to 4.30 pm on
Saturday. To save the cost of call they will call a young
person back.

The National Centre for Eating Disorders
Tel: 0845 838 2040
www.eating-disorders.org.uk

Offers help and advice for parents/carers of young
people.

Families

Kidscape (see page 110 for details)
www.kidscape.org.uk
Email: contact@kidscape.org.uk

Parentline Plus
Tel: 08088 002222
www.parentlineplus.org.uk

The helpline number operates 24 hours a day, 7 days
a week to support parents in all issues of parenting.

Legal advice

Children's Legal Centre
Tel: 0845 456 6811
www.childrenslegalcentre.com
Email: clc@essex.ac.uk

Provides free legal advice regarding children and the law. They have a comprehensive leaflet regarding bullying. The line is open Monday – Friday 9.30 am to 5 pm.

Scottish Child Law Centre
Tel: 0800 328 8970

Provides free legal advice about children and Scottish law. This is a freephone number for children under 18. The line is open Monday – Wednesday and Friday 9.30 am to 4 pm, Thursday 6 to 7.30 pm.

Index

Wise Guides:
helping you deal with whatever life throws at you

Bullying
Michele Elliott

Drugs
Anita Naik

Eating
Anita Naik

Exam Skills
Kate Brookes

Family Break-up
Matt Whyman

Periods
Charlotte Owen

Personal Safety
Anita Naik

Self-Esteem
Anita Naik

Sex
Anita Naik

SELF ESTEEM

Anita Naik

What are you?
Positive bod or negative nerd?
Do you find it hard to take compliments?
Do you never take risks in case you make
a fool of yourself?
Then you need to respect yourself!

Anita Naik gives loads of helpful tips on
how to feel better about yourself and
build your self-esteem. Get in touch with
that positive bod that's just waiting to be
let loose on the world!

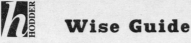

Wise Guide

DRUGS

Anita Naik

What are drugs?
What do they do to your mind –
and your body?
Are you under pressure to take drugs?
Do you have friends who already do?
What are the risks – and how should
you deal with them?

Alcohol and amphetamines, tobacco and
cannabis, solvents and steroids – know
the realities and explode the myths with
this essential wise guide.

Wise Guide

PERSONAL SAFETY

Anita Naik

Are you street smart? Do you step outside feeling confident and secure?

Whatever your outlook one thing is for certain, personal safety is something you can't ignore.

This essential wise guide shows you how to look after yourself when you are out on the street or on the net. Learn how to be more aware of what's going on around you and how to react if you find yourself in a risky situation.